I Look To YOU

An Etoy Bethel Story

JOAN BETHEL

authorHOUSE

AuthorHouse™
1663 Liberty Drive
Bloomington, IN 47403
www.authorhouse.com
Phone: 833-262-8899

Published by AuthorHouse 09/02/2020

ISBN: 978-1-7283-7134-4 (sc)
ISBN: 978-1-7283-7133-7 (hc)
ISBN: 978-1-7283-7132-0 (e)

Library of Congress Control Number: 2020916050

Print information available on the last page.

Any people depicted in stock imagery provided by Getty Images are models,
and such images are being used for illustrative purposes only.
Certain stock imagery © Getty Images.

This book is printed on acid-free paper.

Contents

Acknowledgements

To the All Wise God, Creator, Sustainer, Ruler, Master, Pvider, Healer, Miracle Worker, My All in All for giving me a loving and caring family. For my children and siblings for whatever role you played in taking care of my husband and me – Joan Bethel, Sharon Bethel-Smith, James(Deceased)& Shelley, Jennifer & Lennox Green, Brian & Sharon Bethel, Barrington & Malvease Bethel, Bernard & Jane Bethel, Jacqueline & Ashford Ferguson, Philip & Carlene Bethel, Anya & Allan Dames, Frances Deveaux, Demone Basden. My grandchildren and great grandchildren. My daughter-in-law Sharon Bethel for the countless times back and forth to the hospital with me. My sisters Vernita & Bishop Arnold Josey for taking care of me. My brothers: John, Charles & Godfrey. My sisters: Evangeline, Alice, Angela, Laverne, Betty, Rochelle and, Marilyn. The many persons who prayed for me including my St. John's Church Family, especially Pastor Daniel & Minister Sonia Morlcy, Anniemae Gelin, My nieces & nephews, my offspring's' friends, Essie Deveaux Monica

Lloyd and Gretchen Nelson, Stanton, Candice & Jael, Mother Brezetta Nixon, Former Administrator Everette & Mrs. Hart, Administrator Mr. Theophilus & Mrs. Cox, Administrator: Neil Campbell & Donald Rolle. All doctors at PMH and Western Regional Memorial Centre. Mount Olive Union Baptist Church and Mount Nebo Union Baptist Church, Commonwealth Spiritual Convention & Exuma District Union Convention.

Prologue

Etoy is the beautiful wife of Vincent John Bethel and the proud mother of ten (3) wonderful children – Joan, Sharon, James (Deceased), Jennifer, Brian, Barrington, Bernard, Jacqueline, Philip and Anya and three(3) adopted children, Frances Deveaux, Demone Basden, and Sonia Morley. She is the grandmother of twenty-eight (28) grand-children and the great grandmother of twenty-three (23).

Tribute: Our Mother

Etoy Bethel

The Mother of Elegance, Grace and Charm made her first appearance in this world on 22nd November, 1941. Etoy Bethel is described as a **Proverbs 31 Woman**; her husband Vincent and ten (10) children all 'rise up and call her blessed'. Etoy is a deaconess in her church, St. John's Union Baptist Church. A very strong believer in God, she is a councillor, a prayer warrior and has a passion for the young men of this nation. Etoy Bethel has made her house a home of refuge; her doors are always opened, and many are fed out of her pot.

We can remember as teenagers our mom would transport five (5) gallon buckets filled with water from across the street to the back of our house to full three (3) tubs, one (1) to soak, one (1) to wash and one (1) to rinse. She worked at the Peace n' Plenty Hotel during the day, and during the evening she would bring many guests' clothing home to wash and press. This was done just to make ends meet.

Some evenings she would return to work and turn down beds, making sacrifices for her children. In the year 1990, when our home was destroyed by fire, our mom was our biggest motivator, reminding us that we had each other and those were just earthly possessions destroyed by the fire.

During the year 1993, our mother was admitted to the Princess Margaret Hospital to receive a pacemaker, and from that year until February 2019, our mother has had to replace six (6) pacemakers due to infections from foreign objects in her body. Throughout all the storms in her life, she has not lost her faith, smile, and peace. She is a strong pillar in the St. John's Union Baptist Church, George Town, and indeed in the entire island of Exuma.

We just want to present to you, that person who has and will always be our role model, our covering and mentor. In spite of all she has been through, she continues to hold fast to her faith in God. The text Job 13:15 KJV has become her words of assurance, "Though He slay me, yet will I trust in Him: but I will maintain mine own ways before Him". Our mother is a no nonsense woman, who stands up for what she believes in and 'speaks her mind'. If there is a conflict, she never believes in hearing one side of the story. She would never violate the rights of one child for the other and there is no such thing as being favoured. If you were wrong, she would let you know that you are wrong. Even if it was an adult word over a child, she would take the time to listen to both sides and not just agree with the adult's version. Our mother is a phenomenal woman, a worshipper, a prayer warrior, an intercessor, a councillor, a faithful soldier, with a heart for the youth of our nation.

About the Author

Joey is a Senior Clerk at Administrator's Office,George Town,Exuma,Bahamas.A single mother of three and six grand children.

She received her early childhood education at Rolle Town Primary School, later L.N.Coakley High School ,Prince William High School and Nassau Academy of Business. A active member of St. John"s Baptist Church.

One of her hobbies is reading and was thus inspired by her mother testimonies and her strong faith in God.

Introduction

Bethel Clan

ETOY MALVANIA BETHEL

I was born in the settlement of Hartswell, Exuma, Bahamas, on the 22nd day of November, 1941. My parents were the late Areminia and Leader John Cleveland Rolle. I am the eldest of seven (7) siblings – Rev. Dr. John Sidney Rolle, Minister Evangeline Ingraham, Rev. Dr. Charles Rolle, Alice Rolle,

Deacon Godfrey Rolle and Elder Vernita Josey. I attended the Rolle Town Primary School, and later the Dundas Civic Centre to train in Housekeeping. After leaving the Dundas Civic Centre in 1958, I went to Montagu Hotel to work as a Dishwasher. I grew up in a close knitted loving family. My parents, especially my Dad, were hard working and dedicated. Daddy could not read nor write; however, Mom was able to, and would read for him. My siblings and I grew up in a praying and disciplined home. I accepted Jesus Christ as my Lord and Saviour at the age of eight (8), and from a child had a desire to serve the Lord. During those times, life was good because everybody seemed to love and share with one another. Life was great. My first encounter with sickness was a throat, tonsil, headache and high fever illness. I suffered with this ailment for a long time. In 1958, one of my Aunts attempted to take me to see a doctor. When we reached the clinic, it was closed and we had to go to the doctor's house. The doctor was an army doctor. As the sun was just about to set, and dark fall, she had to use a search light to examine me. She told my aunt that my tonsil was the worse she would have even seen and she sent me to Nassau to take have it removed. Around the end of July, my mother took me to Nassau. I was admitted to the hospital for (3) days. After being discharged from the hospital, mummy and I returned to Exuma. The end of that same year 1958, I got engaged to a handsome young man,

Vincent John Bethel of George Town, Exuma. In 1960, on the 18th July, we were joined in holy matrimony on a Monday afternoon, at Mission Baptist Church, by Rev. Dr. Reuben Cooper Sr. My husband and I lived in Nassau for six (6) years. Our marriage was like any marriage, we had our ups and downs while trying to learn about each other. Sometimes I yearned to be back home.

On 31st August, 1961, our first child was born, Joan Patricia Bethel; our second on 29th January, 1963, Sharon Delores Bethel. Then, I got pregnant again and for some reason mommy came down to Nassau and carried the two (2) girls back to Exuma with her. So, I decided to get a job. Someone told me about a job opening on Mackey Street, so I went and was hired. I worked from eight to four, for a young couple with a baby girl who was just a few months old. I was not there very long. One evening as I got off, I remembered that I did not tell Vincent to take out something to cook. I tried to get home as quickly, but when I reached he was standing in the door. I asked him if he had cooked. He answered 'yes' and while I was standing there a very bad feelings came over me. I sat in the door and while there I thought I would die. I told Vincent how I felt and asked him to make me some peppermint tea while I went to lay down. I could not go back to work due to my pregnancy sickness. I prayed to feel better, but got worst.

After having our first son, my husband and his uncle

named him Vincent James Bethel, He was born on the 26th June, 1964. It was one of the rainiest season around that time. Only God knew how we made it. Our stove was in our uncle's house, and we had to go outside next door. All day the baby and I was home during the rain, thunder and lightning. I had to be back and forth to doctor. They could not tell what was wrong with me. Some said it was my nerve, some said meningitis, and all the while, my health was worsening. My head would be spinning, I could not look up nor bow my head. All I would do were pray and cry; it was only me my God and my baby, until Vincent came home.

My friends it was a very hard and rough time for me. Some of my aunts would pass by and ask how I was doing, I could not explain I. Sometimes it would feel like dead weight and a hollow in my lower chest. I don't know how I made it; but I can say without a shadow of a doubt, it was only God. Three (3) months after James was born, I found out I was pregnant with my fourth child Jennifer Amanda. I did not know how I would make it, because I was still sick. After a year and some, I asked my husband to go back home for a while, and he told me we could go. We went and were there for about two weeks. My mother went down to Nassau, and when she came back, Vincent came too. He left everything we had at home. I started feeling much better in November 1966. I was able to work

over the years during my other pregnancies. I did my best taking care of the children, with the help of my parents and my mother in-laws. I made it. When I moved in our home in George Town the four (4) older children stayed with my mother. I had Bernard the very night after we moved in George Town in our home. Bernard was born in 1971, and he was christened at St. Johns Baptist Church. So I went back to work. Jacqueline Yvette was born 3rd May, 1973. Philip Deon was born 5th January, 1976. When I got pregnant with my last child Anya Shenique I did not have much energy. When I went for my first check-up the nurse informed me that I had to go to Nassau to have the baby. I left 25th September, and had her on 25th November, it was a very rough time and I was extremely painful. I was living with my brother and sister in-law Charles and Lavern. My brother would always encourage me saying, "Sis it isn't long now". Daddy came down to see me, I believe on a Sunday, he and left via boat on a Wednesday and I began experiencing a slight nipping pain while he was there. Saturday I visited my Sister Vangy and that's when the pain begin coming on hotter. She took me back home to my brother's house. I took a bath, made some thyme tea, and by 9: 00. p.m. I woke my brother up. He took me to the hospital after 10:00 p.m., and she never came until 1:45a.m Sunday morning. I was so weak I started to haemorrhage.

The hospital called my husband to give consent to

have me 'tied off', which he did. On the following Sunday morning I woke up with a high fever and swollen breast. While at home, my sister-in-law Betty came to visit me and called Dr. Gray, her cousin, after she was concerned about my appearance. He told her to take me to the hospital, where he will meet us. He came there and examined my breast. He told us it was abscess and it had to be amputated. The following week, that Monday, I went into surgery. When the surgery was completed, they sent me home and every other day I had to go on the ward for the doctor to check my cut. That was around late November through December 1979 and it was cold. One day the nurse in the dressing room said, "Lady you soon go home"; however, that same night I did not sleep well due to the pain.

On the following morning I went to the ward. When the Doctor came he asked how I was doing and I told him that I did not sleep for pain. He went to check his other patients on the ward and came back to me. Again, I told him that I was in pain. He took a tweezer and lifted the bottom part of the cut and the pus came flowing out. That morning I was so cold. I left the ward in pain and went to ECG where my baby sister Vernita worked and asked her for a cup of tea. They had no sugar, or teabags. I told her to give me the hot water. I had the chills and drank the hot water without anything in it. I had to wait out front for my other sister to take me home. and in spite of it, I kept trusting in my God.

I went back to work. While my mother-in-law kept the baby. When I was away, my late Aunt, Satara, told me that one day Barrington, being a little boy, asked if his mummy was coming back. That made me feel so bad because I never left my children. In the 1980s I felt that I wanted to get closer to the Lord. I prayed and asked God, and He began to open His Word. And I felt His presence anew. At the end of the year 1989, I felt God presence stronger even when I knelt to pray at home or in church. It felt like someone was present with me. I look and there is no one. And I would say that it is God. In 1990, as that year began, I thanked the Lord and told the people that this is a package and every day it will unfold.

Chapter One

Have you ever been in storms that keep on coming; when one finishes, there is another one in the making. Well I just want to encourage you that storms of life will come at you and if you are not rooted and grounded in the Solid Rock, you will crumble and fall and stay down. Just want to share a few of the storms that tried to keep me down. But I give thanks unto God because I am here and I'm still standing and holding on to His hand. Satan thought he had me, but thanks be to God who says in John 10: 28 KJV, "And I give unto them eternal life; and they shall never perish, neither shall any man pluck them out of my hand".

When I made my entrance, this side of paradise, it was 20th November, 1941. This was the date my mommy told me; but it was recorded in the Birth Registry as 22nd November, 1941. My parents Areminia and John Cleveland Rolle, both deceased, were the couple God created for me to be the first blessed seed of their loins. I am the eldest of seven (7) siblings – Rev. Dr. John Sidney Rolle, Minister Evangeline Ingraham-Fowler, Rev Dr. Charles Rolle, Deaconess Alice

Rolle, Deacon Godfrey Rolle and Elder Vernita Josey. We grew up a close knitted loving family. My parents, especially my Dad, were hard working and dedicated. Daddy could not read nor write. Mummy could manage to read, so she would try to read. The words he did not know, we would pronounce for him. My siblings and I grew up in a praying and disciplined home. I accepted Jesus as my Lord and Saviour at the age of eight (8), and had a desire to serve the Lord. Growing up as a teenager I knew I was blessed and highly favoured. I realize that every morning as soon as I awake, the enemy is on the attack. He will try everything in his power to discourage the saints. He will do everything to make them feel weak and lonely. He will remind them that their health is failing and that they are getting old.

You see the devil takes no vacation, he takes no holidays, he takes no break, and there is no time out for him. That is the reason 1 Peters 5:8 NIV says, "Be alert and of sober mind. Your enemy the devil prowls around like a roaring lion looking for someone to devour". I come to the realization that every morning is an opportunity for me to feel God's presence, mercy and amazing grace. I have made up my mind not to let disappointments get the best of me. I won't let problems fester. I won't allow Satan to hold my future hostage.

Chapter Two

I can remember as if it was yesterday, 20th April, 1990, around 6:30 p.m. It was a Friday, the last week before the 22nd Annual National Family Island Regatta. My children were making preparation for other members of the family to visit. My eldest child had gotten a loan from the bank to purchase a front room set. The kitchen had just been renovated, with new appliances, and there was ample space for more than eight (8) persons to hold in the kitchen at the same time without bumping into each other. Our cupboards were filled, as we had just purchased our wholesale groceries which came on the mail boat. That season, I had an abundance of dry peas in stock. One of my daughters was in the kitchen cooking a big pot of crab and rice and baked chicken, because we had thirteen (13) family members at home at that time. We were preparing for more family members to arrive for the Regatta. Two (2) of my children had not too long returned from a trip to the USA, whereas they had shopped for other family members as well for the upcoming Regatta. I can still hear my son

Barrington, saying that he smells something burning, coming from the east side where three (3) of the bedrooms were located. He along with my eldest got up to investigate whether someone had used the iron and accidently left it on. When they checked the iron was unplugged, but still we smelt smoke and fire.

They decided to check the master bedroom, and lo to our surprise, the clothes on the right left side of my closet was engulfed in flame. Fire was coming from the ceiling and my son Barrington ran to get a bucket of water to douse the fire. I ran across the street at the Silver Dollar Restaurant & Bar to call for help. After my son threw the bucket of water on the fire, the fire spread quicker, and we immediately rounded up all of the children playing on the floor and took them on the outside, My son picked up all of his new clothes which he had just purchased and rest them on the west side patio of the house. My daughter picked up the suitcase with my second offspring baby items, because she was now expecting her second child and had sent away for baby items. She carried this suitcase on the outside of the house, but apparently the beam of the house fell on the suitcase and everything was destroyed. It took approximately 10 minutes for the entire house to burn down. Our family lost every earthly possession we had that day, including our neighbour's home.

We later learned that it was an electrical fire. We lost all of our material things in that fire, except the clothes that were on our backs. We were left with just memories. No family albums to look back over the different stages of our lives. I was also holding asue money at that time. I often tell people that our home went down in grand style, fully equipped. A fire engine was dispatched to the scene, but the truck had no water. It seems like in 10 minutes our house burnt right down to the ground. This was a season of separation for us. We were always a close knitted family, because we enjoyed each other's company. One of my daughter who was preparing to enter the College of the Bahamas that same semester had to live with my husband's sister. My last daughter went to live with her god-mother. I gave thanks and recognition to the late Mr. Samuel Gray, who gave us one of his cottages at Mount Pleasant, rent free, for months. Some of my children had nightmares of that fire. We had persons who just poured into us, spiritually and financially.

The entire Exuma Community was there to give their support. You know persons usually say they receive more than what they had before, Well, trust me, you can never replace family portraits and memories that you shared in the past, with familiar possessions that can never be regained. I must say that St. John's Family was there for us.

A fire Relief Fund was set up at the Bank of Nova Scotia by the late Rev. L. E. Moss and Rev. E.J. Rolle to assist with the building of a new home. But through it all we are still a family who believed in prayers. In six months' time, we were back together in our newly built home, which we are still dwelling in to date. I refer to it as the home which God built. Regardless of who visits our home, they will just make themselves comfortable and will tell us to 'run' them home. A home is filled with Love, Laughter and Life. Three of my daughters who are married and living here on the island, will always find themselves every evening after work to hang out before going home. Our Yard is referred to as the 'Big Yard', all the grandkids hang there, thus attracting others to hang out there as well. Over the years, I have come to believe that our home is a 1 Corinthians 3: 16 CSB, 'Don't you yourselves know that you are God's temple and that the Spirit of God lives in you?' I believe that is the reason so many visitors alike keep returning to our home, because of the presence of God resides there. There is a song that says, 'with Christ in your vessel you can smile at the storm'. It is very easy to repeat that phrase but to actually live it is a challenge.

Chapter Three

There were days I just did not feel like smiling. Yes Philippians 4:11 KJV states, 'Not that I speak in respect of want; for I have learned, in whatsoever state I am, therewith to be content'. It was a struggle to go out some days, because some of the clothing received were too big and others were unusable. But you could not complain because you had to be grateful for all the help that was given. In September 1993. I began to complain of feeling tired and drain all the time. I went to our local clinic in George Town and was seen by the medical doctor, who advised me to go into Nassau for a check-up, because the heart rating was very weak. Preparation was made for me to travel into Nassau to receive the check-up.

After seeing the doctor in Princess Margaret Hospital who diagnosed that the bottom section of my heart had deteriorated, I was admitted right away into the Intensive Care Unit. I was informed that I had to have a pacemaker installed and a specialist had to be flown in to assist with the surgery, because it was a risky one. When my children received the news back in Exuma that I had to be admitted to ICU and was not well at all, it was like a death blow to the Bethel household in Exuma. This operation was costly and my children helped to plan a steak out to assist with medical bills. There was a cook out in Exuma also to assist with my medical bill. A lot of prayers and fasting went up on my behalf for full recovery. I came through this operation because of God's grace and mercy.

This was the first scar I received. Although the surgery was a success, the road to recovery was very tedious. The prescriptions that were prescribed at the time was too strong and had a very negative affect on my system. There were days I was unable to get out of the bed. In the midst of all this upheaval and rough period in my life, I still held on to my faith and my God. I went back to the doctor; but still the situation was the same, there were no changes. Even after visiting the doctor for some time, just when he said that I could go home, the next morning which was Sunday I began vomiting and feeling disoriented. My baby sister Vernita Josey called the doctor and was advised to make an appointment to the Centerville Diagnostics Centre to have a gall bladder test.

This torture went on for a few months. It wasn't until my daughter Sharon called one day and suggested that they take me to the clinic in Lyford Cay to seek further help for my condition. It was there that I discovered the medications' dosages that were given to me by the previous doctor, too strong for my system. After the dosages were decreased I began to improve in my health. This was a next battle Satan lost. He doesn't understand that my help comes from the Lord, and in God alone I stand.

Chapter Four

The bible declares that weeping may endure for a night but joy comes in the morning. I had to hold fast to this belief. There were times when my tears flowed like a running tap. It was during the year 1997 when my baby girl was accepted to the Royal Bahamas Police Force and began her training at the Police College. The enemy stepped in and interrupted the plans God had set out for her. My baby was always the life of the party, so when she became listless and depressed everyone knew something was wrong. She would go into a deep depression, high level of anxiety, agitation and constant crying. She was under a very heavy attack. It was impossible to sleep at night because she could not sleep. She would just cry and at that time I had to take her to various doctors to diagnose her.

There were days when she would just fall upon my shoulders and burst out crying for no apparent reason. It seemed like this nightmare would never end. She would cry, then she would sing and pray, but yet the fears and tears persisted. There was no joy and laughter, just the feeling of hopelessness and helplessness. This affected the whole family. I was physically, mentally and emotionally drained. She constantly had to be watched to make sure she was alright.

Day after day, month after month, this constant battling of her mind, spirit and body, began to take a toll on myself and other family members. In order for me to get some rest, my daughter had to spend some nights at one of my adopted daughters who was a prayer warrior Viola Deveaux (Deceased). Later she was sent to my sister and brother, Bishop Arnold and Elder Vernita Josey in New Providence. After so many trips back and forth to then doctor, it was later discovered that my baby had active thyroid, and required surgery. But for the Grace of God, my child is now in her sound mind and did not have to be institutionalized as the enemy wanted to destroy her. To God be the glory, great things he hath done! Amidst all that I went through, I am still here, still standing. Even when the enemy attacked me again in 2016, the God in whom we serve is well able to deliver and He did again. Our God of Second Chances is greatly to be praised. Praise be to God My daughter is now married and is the proud mother of two handsome sons. She can look back over her life and can testify of God's abundance grace and mercy, that has allowed her to come thus far by faith. With the help of Almighty God and the support and love from family and acquaintances, I can truly say that God is indeed God, there is none else that compare to Him. He is always an on time God. When you feel like there is no way out, no hope, no help, no joy, no fulfilment, just emptiness and brokenness, God is right in the midst of all that craziness going on in your mind and He steps in. When you lose control and can't take any more, He moves on your behalf. That's the God my parents, John Cleveland and Aremina Rolle served. The same God Abraham, Isaac and Jacob served. The God who delivered the three Hebrew boys out of the fiery furnace, the God who allowed Moses to part the Red Sea, is still the same God we are worshipping today.

There is no God who can compare to Jehovah, our God. Every other gods are idols, and they have to bow to the Holy One of Israel. God has brought me through many dangers, toils and snares. So I don't have anything else to do but worship and trust Him. If I decide to run from His spirit and hide from His presence, He will still find me. So I made up my mind come what may, I will trust Him until the day I die. Even though pain rock this body of mine, and I have had go through numerous surgeries, I will speak like Habakkuk, "When the fig tree does not bud, and there are no grapes on the vines; when the olive trees do not produce, and the fields yield no crops; when the sheep disappear from the pen, and there are no cattle in the stalls, I will rejoice because of the LORD; I will be happy because of the God who delivers me!" (Habakkuk 3:17-18 NET).

Chapter Five

It was in the year 2000 when I became ill again and had to go into Nassau to seek medical help. It was discovered that the pacemaker was extremely low and had to be replaced. The warranty on it was not even expired as yet; but here it is again, I have to go through the same procedure, with another operation to install a new pacemaker because the previous pacemaker's battery was extremely low. I cannot began to describe to you the suffering I went through with pain wrecking my body. This was another journey back into Nassau to go through more tests and x-rays, more blood works and the likes. I went through this operation successfully. In all of this I continued to give thanks to God for allowing me to bear my cross with a smile. Life has not been easy, but I will press my way through the dark clouds.

I constantly say that my ten (10) children are my only investment I have here on this side. I believe in not giving up on God, regardless of how much time the adversary works overtime to try and make me feel that my Heavenly Father had abandoned me. I knew beyond a shadow of a doubt that my God would see me through, even when I felt like I was going under. Mercy said no once again to the four D's that will drag you under – Death, Defeat, Depression and Discouragement. I, not only trusted in my God, but held on firm. There were days when I felt that God had taken a vacation from me, but I always remembered the verse in Isaiah 41:10 ESV, "Fear not for I am with you, be not dismayed for I am your God. I will strengthened you, I will help you, and I will uphold you with My righteous right hand". I know that every morning as soon as I awake, the enemy is on the attack, he will try everything in his power to discourage the saints, he will do everything to make you feel weak and lonely. He will remind you that your health is failing and you are getting old.

You see the devil takes no vacation, he takes no holidays, he takes no breaks, and there is no time out for him. That is the reason 1 Peters 5:8 says "Be alert and sober minded your enemy, the devil prowls around like a roaring lion looking for someone to devour". I realize that every morning is an opportunity for me to feel God's presence, mercy and amazing grace. As a child of God I have made up my mind not to let disappointments get the best of me. I won't let problems fester, and I won't allow Satan to hold my future hostage.

Chapter Six

I am a prayer warrior and Satan's worst enemy. When he realized that every time he knocked me down, God brought me up with more vigour and strength than before, he decided to change his tactics. In 2002 there was an occurence that happened . I was devasted and poured out my heart to God. I literally questioned why me Lord of my, In this fiery trial, the song that came to mind was, "Why me Lord, what have I ever done to deserve, even one, of the pleasures, I've known, Tell me Lord what did I ever do that was worth loving you. All the kindness you showed. Lord help me Jesus I've wasted it so, help me Jesus, I know what I am, now that I know that I've needed you so, help me Jesus my soul's in your hand". That road I pray, I never walk again.

You see around that time there were young girls in the family,. H could the enemy be so bold to come on the premises and touch one, even though they were covered with the Blood of Jesus and every morning before they left home for school, I would pray over them and anoint them with oil? But I had to go through that season of anguish, and I can testify today, that all we have to do is to put our trust in Jesus and expect him to do the rest. In spite of this painful situation I was able to see God's hand over my family and he healed that period of grief I was going through. I had to let go and let God be God. I begun to thank Him with tears streaming down my face many days, I gave him my pain. Let me just encourage someone who maybe going through your season of grief and feeling abandoned. Our God is still omnipresent still omnipotent, still omniscient. He is carrying you when you cannot feel Him or trace Him.

Chapter Seven

The proverbs is so true which states, "Many are the afflictions of the righteous but the Lord delivers him out of them all" Proverbs 34:19 ESV. When you look at these words you can truly say without any doubt that whatever you go through with Jesus on your side, you will make it. It was March 2014 during the period for the Exuma District Union Convention, both my husband and I took ill and had to go to Nassau to seek further medical help. This was a very dark period in my family's life that they had to face because both of us kept blacking out and the doctor's report was everything was well and they could not find the reason why the fainting spells were occurring. But at the end of the day things were not well because we both continued to have dizzy spells and would continue to black out.

This went on for almost a month and we had to remain in Nassau to see the doctor and determine what was going on with us. The song writer says, "Through many danger toils and snares I have already come, His grace has bought me safe this far and His grace will lead me on". Eventually we came home, and we were still going through. I recalled the late Apostle Rodney Roberts from Five Porches Church, Nassau, sent two of his armour bearer to come to Exuma and do warfare on our behalf. Through many prayers and giving God thanks for a miracle, I can truthfully say that God did it again. He allowed both of us to survive that attack that was sent. We were delivered from the hands of the enemy.

The dizziness and the fainting spell stopped. 'God is able to do what He says He will do. He's going to fulfil every promises to you. Don't give up on God, because He won't give up on you. He is able to do exceedingly, abundantly above all we can ask, think or imagine". It was rough, but don't give up on God, He knows what is best for us and it is not over until God says it is over. Looking through the natural eyes. It seems like it was the end for us. It was like a hopeless situation, you are there but cannot make the situation better. You just have to pray and endure. In all of this I believe God was a Keeper and He still is. He said whatever we present to Him, He will keep it. I know that my God can do all things exceedingly, abundantly above all I can ask, think or imagine. He is just that kind of God.

Chapter Eight

There were days when it seems like nothing was going right. It seems like a dark cloud was over my head and had me literally disconnected from myself. It felt like I was just going through the motions. I just felt tired and weary and felt like throwing in the towel. It was like a merry-go round, just spinning around in the same circle. Even when I did not feel the presence of God, I knew deep down inside of me that He was still there. He had to be there because His word says, "I will never leave you or forsake you". I tried so hard to encourage myself; But I often felt so drained by just trying to be strong and courageous. I had poured so much out and here I am in this season feeling like I am in an isolated place, and I am stuck. I am going to church, but still yearning to be completely passionate for the things of Christ. God is not a man that He shall lie, so in the midst of my weakest hour, I knew He still had me covered. Every day I awoke, it was to discover that I was alive. At times not giving thanks and praise had me feeling weighed down. Even thou the bible say that many are the afflictions of the righteous, the Lord delivered them out of it all, the spirit of torment was upon me and there were nights I could not sleep. I would just sit on my bed and groan.

This was reassurance for me, but I still worried why me Lord. I had to go back to the doctor and was admitted to the hospital. The report was the wires from the pacemaker was infected and thus I ended up with a bad case of the diarrhoea for three solid weeks. Eight (8) times a day I would be passing out green stool. The back and forth twice a day to PMH was very tiresome at times. It was really an experience to stand still and see what God was up to. There were days when Mr. Doubt would visit and have me to believe that I wasn't getting better. The pain I was going through was unbearable. I loved food and for several weeks I could not even eat. When I was released from the hospital after four (4) weeks, I still could not eat. I had no appetite for almost two (2) months and had lost a lot of weight. But God saw me through this.

Chapter Nine

The enemy was and still is after me and my family. On Saturday 30th August, 2010,one (1) of my daughters and her two (2) daughters were asleep in her bedroom, when an intruder came through one of the front room window. Heentered the bedroom and began touching my thirteen year old granddaughter's back. You see the enemy will try every tactic, every scheme to try and get you to lose focus on what God has in store for you. He wants you not to trust the God, who protects. You see, my daughter had an assignment for that Sunday to minister at a local church. I can say without a shadow of a doubt, that night they were in the Potter's Hand. The enemy walked in and had to step over the bible that was still on the floor that my daughter was using. God allowed his angels to be dispatched so that no harm could befall them. The enemy came in through the window and walked out through the door and I can truly say that if God is not on our side where will be.

Our God still protects, heals, delivers, and provides, He still makes rough paths smooth, and crooked paths straight.

He is still a bridge over troubled water. He still speaks peace in the midst of a storm. He is still a way out of no way. He's still a balm in Gilead. He's still a shield, a refuge, a fortress, a present help in any trouble. I've learn how to lean and to trust in Jesus. He is a friend to the friendless, a mother to the motherless and a husband to the widow. Our God is awesome! He is wonderful. He is lawyer in the courtroom and a doctor in the theatre. He is just beautiful in every situation. I've tried Him over and over and He is just alright. He keeps me in perfect peace. He give me strength to make it through the day. The hymn writer describes so well the song, "I've found a friend, oh such a friend He loves me, ere I knew Him. He drew me with his cords of love and thus He bound me to Him. And round my heart so closely twine those ties which naught can sever, for I am His and He is mine forever and forever". He's my friend, comforter, Saviour, King, Lord, and battle-axe. He is my God and in him will I trust.

He kept me from my enemies when they come up against me like a flood. My God lifts up His standards and hide me under His wings. He gives me joy in times of sorrow. He keeps my heart and my mind stayed on Him. There is no one else like Jesus. No one else can touch my heart the way He does. He is my Yesterday, Today and Tomorrow. He is all I need. I live to serve Him and to give Him glory. When billows rise, He keeps my soul. My God, My Heavenly Father, He watches over me. I trust Him completely with all that I have and all that I am.

Chapter Ten

In 2012 thru 2014, this was a season of great distresss, depression and torment, when one . family member is under attack, it affects the whole family. This child of mine was in a state of limbo, and was depressed, tormented, distraught, and full with anxiety, fearfulness and Insomnia. . I will never even wish this on my enemy to endure. The whole family was going through this ordeal There were many night that I could not sleep, because she had to lay in the bed with me, just twisting and turning and she could not sleep. She went to doctors, and she tried sleeping pills but still could not sleep.

She would constantly lay on my shoulder and just cry. We prayed, we cry, we read the bible in her hearing, but the situation did not chang . For over three and half years we took care of her and prayed to God to intervene and make what was wrong right. But our time is not God's time. We wanted instant, but you see God has plan for all of our lives, and there has to be process before there can be progress. I knew that God would change the situation; but I did not know how or when. So I continued to trust Him for it. In spite of the dark days, sleepless night and crying out to God for release for the child that he had loan, I still believed that God is an on time God. It may seem like forever and that the situation turn from bad to worse; But I comforted myself in knowing that the God in whom I serve made me a promise that He wouldn't put more on me than I can bear. One song writer penned the words, "Must Jesus bear the cross alone and all the whole go free. No there is a cross for everyone and there's a cross for me. The consecrated cross I'll bear till death shall set me free. Then go on my crown to wear, for there's a crown for me". It was rough, and some days my spirit was low but I had to cast all my cares upon the God who made me in His image and in his likeness. Trusting Him for each day I face, believing that this too shall pass. I reflected on Job and all that he had possessed. He lost everything but still held on to his faith in God. So I had to remind myself and let Satan know that in spite of the fiery trials, I am determined to hold on until the end, because Jesus is all I have, and I am depending on Him to bring us through the tests. Today my daughter is a living testimony that God is still able to do exceeding abundantly above all I can think, ask or even imagine. He delivered her out of her misery and suffering. He can do it for you too whatever you are going through.

Chapter Eleven

In December 2018, I took ill again, and began having chills and at the same time high fever. I was admitted to Princess Margaret Hospital again. While on the Female Surgical Ward, one of my nieces had to be flown in on emergency flight and was admitted on the same ward as myself in January 2019. Unfortunately, she died the same day they brought her to the ward. This was a blow because she was like a daughter to me. She stayed in my home. At this time the doctors at Princess Margaret said that there was nothing else they could do for me to get well and had a meeting with some of my family and suggested they seek further medical help in the U.S.A. My first born son, James Vincent Bethel instructed my eldest daughter not to wait for the Homecoming Service of my niece and their cousin, but to make arrangement for me to go to the U.S.A. He had already made arrangements with his sisters in the U.S.A.

We went to the U.S.A on 31st January, 2019. I went to a heart Specialist on 1st February, 2019, . After consultation and examination, the doctor informed my children that if I had waited a few day more, I would have died. He looked at me and knew what I had already known. I had called my children and told them to release me, because I knew I was dying. The infection had already spread through my body and had entered the valve of the heart. I was admitted that same day to the Intensive Care Unit of Westside Regional Medical Centre.

I had to undergo another surgery to replace another pacemaker and to remove five wires that were left in me from previous pacemakers. This was causing me so much anguish. The operation was a success, but it was uphill because of the infection through my body, I had to stay in the hospital for three (3) weeks on heavy antibiotics. My son James, daughter-in-law Shelley and daughter Joan, two adopted daughters Monica and Gretchen were there with me throughout the process. It was a long journey regaining my health and strength. I ended up with blood clots in my two legs while I was in the Hospital and now have to take blood thinners as advised by doctor, for the rest of my life. But my God is well able to do far more that I can imagine. I had to take needles twice a day in my stomach and had to use a calibrator. I had to learn how to walk again. My son James was the drill sergeant, and he would make sure I do a few laps around the pool, so that I did not have to go in rehab. While I was healing and making preparation to come back home, my son James began feeling sick.

Chapter Twelve

My first born son, started experiencing pain in his stomach and his shoulders. He went to the doctor and had numerous test. When I left the U.S.A. in March, my son stayed behind to see the doctor. He was able to go back to Freeport on 30th March, 2019. He was still not 100 percent. His wife was not pleased with the way he looked, so she took him back to the doctor. He was admitted to the Rand Hospital for a few days on 4th April, then his wife took him back to the U.S.A. where he was admitted to Westside Regional Medical Centre, where I had previously spent about four (4) weeks. He was there for about eight (8) days.

He went back home to Grand Bahama, and had to be airlifted on 7th June, 2019, to Broward Health Medical Centre. He was there for three (3) weeks. I was prayed and asked God to heal my son. This son of mine was the one who got up to fix my breakfast and lunch every morning and evening when I was released from hospital. He was there to encourage me, and to hold my hand and walk with me, because he did not want them to put me in Rehab. On

4th July, 2019, my loving, dedicated and caring son passed away. Saints of God let me tell you if I had the power to go and he stayed, I would have done it in a heartbeat. But it was not my lot to understand the wisdom of God to take the son who cared for me throughout my illness, and left me who battled illness all my life.

When I received the news that Thursday morning that my darling son passed away, it felt like it was just a nightmare I had to awaken from. The Bible taught us that weeping may endure for a night but joy comes in the morning. It felt like morning will never appear. My grief was so heavy. I awoke every morning crying, this was one storm I did not want to face. I had to continually ask God forgiveness and tell Him I was at His mercy and needed His grace to make it through, because I could not face this without His strength. On Friday 26th July, 2019, my son was laid to rest at St. John's Jubilee Cathedral, Freeport. Amidst the pain and heartbreak, I was happy in my spirit to know that James was at peace and resting with my Lord and Saviour Jesus Christ. He lived a life that was pleasing in the sight of God. My heart still aches some days when my mind rest on him, because of the calibre of man that he was. He is greatly missed.

Chapter Thirteen

I realized that the devil doesn't bother with people if they don't have anything going on. He just kept coming back. After living in George Town for over 50 years, the enemy raised his ugly head again .but God will reveal who are your enemies aretbut. Saints when I say the devil is like a roaring lion seeking soul he may devour; he is always up to his tricks. The enemy will walked into the yard . And destroy what belongs to you. However, thanks be to God who gives me the victory to know that I am more than a conqueror. It grieves my heart to see people not concerned about their one soul, but to be obsessed over land that we will all have to leave one day. God knows I try to live a life that is pleasing in His sight, and to do unto others as I would have them do unto me. I even to love those who despitefully use me. I know greater is coming for the turmoil and the test I had to endure. I can surely declare that God is still on His throne, He sees every tear drop and He hears every groan and sigh. He promises that He will give me the garment of praise, for the spirit of heaviness; He will give me the oil of joy, for the spirit of mourning.

Can I tell you when God blesses you, no man can curse you. Opposition might rise up, darts come from unexpected directions, but you see, the God in whom I serve, He is a deliverer. He has always been on my side, and nothing can separate me from His love. Though the storm clouds rise and darkness is all around, yet will I trust in the ever present help in times of trouble. I have to make a difference in the lives of my children and others around me. I have to let my light shine so that men can see my good works and glorify my Father in heaven. The bible says that when the enemy comes in like a flood the Spirit of God will lift up a standard. I have to testify saints that the Spirit of God has lifted up that standard time after time. In my walk with God, I've had to lift my head high, even when my enemies try to slay me. I trusted in the source of my strength. God promises that He won't put on us more than we can bear. I had to turn the other cheek when a child of God, a man of the God looked me in the face and asked me if I believe that I am the only one saved. This hurt my feelings, but I can truly say that no one will steal my joy. Because, this joy that I have, the world did not give it to me, and the world can't take it away.

I am standing on the promises of God, regardless of what negativity is thrown at me. I am saved because I confess Jesus Christ as Lord of my life and I believe that He is the Son of God. He was born, He died and rose, and now He is sitting at the right hand of God the Father making intercession for us. As I look back over my life, I can truly say that I am a testimony. This world is not my home and I am just a pilgrim in this land. Through many dangers toils and snares I have already come. God's amazing grace, His bountiful mercies are renewed to me every morning. I join in with the hymn writer, Philip P. Bliss, when he penned the words, "I am so glad that my Father in heaven, tells of His love in the book He has given. Wonderful things in the Bible I see, this is the dearest that Jesus loves me. I am so glad that Jesus loves me, Jesus love me, Jesus love me. I am so glad that Jesus loves me. Jesus loves even me". Psalms 34:19 ESV says, "Many are the afflictions of the righteous, but the Lord delivers him out of them all." Yes, I have scars over my body from the many surgeries I had to undergo which were painful. However, when I reflect on the scars Jesus endured for mankind, He who had no sin, but took on my sin and the entire human race's, all I can say, like the prophet Isaiah, "But He was wounded for our transgressions, He was bruised for our iniquities. The chastisement of our peace was upon Him and by His stripes..." (Isaiah 53:5 MEV) I declare that I am heal. Jehovah Ropha is still at work. He is still the Balm in Gilead. He is still the Repairer of the Breach, and Restorer of the Path to Dwell in. I am not seeking favour from mankind on earth. I am seeking the favour of God. I am bought with a price that is very priceless. It's far above rubies, diamonds, emerald or gold. You may be talked about, looked down upon, despised and rejected; but if you have King Jesus in the depths of your soul, come what may, you will make it. Troubles don't last always. The sun will shine, the clouds will roll away, the dawn will break, the mountain will be removed, the broken heart will be mended, the weak will be strengthened, and the captive can be set free.

Come what may I am sticking with Jesus. He has done so much for me. I can tell of His goodness and greatness. I am determined to hold out to the end. Jesus is with me, and on Him I truly can depend. Joshua 24:15 NLT says, "But if you refuse to serve the LORD, then choose today whom you will serve. Would you prefer the gods your ancestors served beyond the Euphrates? Or will it be the gods of the Amorites in whose land you now live? But as for me and my family, we will serve the LORD." I made up in my mind many years ago to do as Joshua did – serve the God that my ancestors served. If none stand with me, I'll stand alone with Jesus. I am still here, but for the grace of God. He is my Sovereign Lord, my battle, my shade by day and defence by night. He covers me. My Creator, my Master, my Father. My Saviour. He's my captain, my pilot, my chauffeur, my guide, my protector, my provider, my deliverer, my healer, my haven of rest, my secret place, my Redeemer and friend. My faith has found a resting place and that is in Jesus alone. The bills keep coming, but I will trust Him. I have to make trips into the US.A and Nassau for check-ups but I will trust Him. The bills astronomical high, but I will trust Him. I don't know what else to do, but to trust in God who made me.

Chapter Fourteen

I can recall during Tropical Storm Matthew, My husband and I both were in Nassau attending doctor. My sister and her husband were attending a revival that week. One night I went with them even though I still was not feeling well. It was raining constantly, while we were in service. After service was over the road was flooded with water, and many vehicles were stalled in the road. Bishop car was able to drive to a nearby area, the water was almost knee high, I remember stepping out of the car and I don't know what happened after that. I found myself flat on the ground. But God allowed me not to fall in the water but on dry ground.

So I am still here to encourage someone by the grace of God to hold on Jesus. He never told us the journey would be easy. He never told us the burdens will not get heavy. He never told us the storm would not rage. He never told us there will always be sunshine. He never told us there will be no rain. He never said there will be no sorrow. He never said there will be no pain. But He did promise that He will be with us to the very end. So no matter what we go through, no matter how we feel, God is always on our side. In the midst of your fiery furnace, He promises that He will never leave us, nor forsake us. Regardless of what you face, what you have to endure, God promises that nothing can separate us from His love.

When Satan counted me out, God said, "Oh no, there is still a yet praise deep inside of her, for Me to be glorified. So my encouragement to you is that whatever breath you take, praise God for He doesn't owe us any favours. As a matter of fact we owe it all to Him, for His unfailing love and faithfulness He bestows on us day by day.

Conclusion

My Father, Our God, Jehovah, Great I am, I am that I am, Wonderful Al mighty God, Everlasting Father, Prince of Peace, Lord I exalt You, I honour You, I lift Your Name on high. Your Name is above every name. At the N of Jesus, every knee shall bow and every tongue shall confess that Jesus Christ is Lord to the glory of God. I just want to express my gratitude, appreciation and thanks to Almighty God for being with me throughout all the changing scenes of life. Lord you knew me before I was conceived in my mother's womb. You know the plans you had for me. I think of James every day and my heart aches, when I remember those precious moments. I did not know they would be our last together.

Looking back now, I can say my God is so awesome. He gave us that time where he spent his last caring for me. I give God thanks for his life and knowing one day I will see him again. My prayers and thanks go out to Shelly and the children, Joan whom the heavy lot falls on and all of the children, my daughter Sharon, Brian's wife, my siblings who were concerned, Mother Nixon who always calls, almost every day.

One of these getting up morning, I will be done with all the travelling back and forth to doctors, all the surgeries, all the check-ups, all the bills, all the heartache, all the pain. Where I am going, there will be no more sickness, no more crying, no more pain, because Jesus promise me a home over there. He said in John 14:3 KJV, "And if I go and prepare a place for you, I will come again, and receive you unto Myself; that where I am, there ye may be also." Etoy can say undeniably that, "My faith has found a resting place, not in device nor creed. I trust the Ever living One, His wounds for me shall plead. I need no other argument, I need no other plea, it is enough that Jesus died, and that He died for me. My heart is leaning on the Word, the written Word of God. Salvation by my Saviour's Name, Salvation through His blood. My great Physician heals the sick. The lost He came to save. For me His precious blood He shed. For me His life He gave. I need no other argument, I need no other plea. It is enough that Jesus died and that He died for me". When I see Jesus it will be AMEN!

Printed in the United States
By Bookmasters